ABOUT THE AUTHOR

Stefan Mohamed is a performing poet, author and creative writing tutor based in Bristol. He is the author of the *Bitter Sixteen Trilogy* and *Falling Leaves* (Salt Publishing), spoken word collection *PANIC!* (Burning Eye Books) and poetry pamphlet *The Marketplace of Ideas* (Stewed Rhubarb).

Find out more than you ever wanted to know about him at www.stefmo.co.uk

"In *Farewell Tour*, Stefan Mohamed takes us on a hellish road trip through the psyche of a mean and defeated nation. It is hard to think of a poet who goes further in creating a new poetic register from materials not usually found in poetry. The language of *Farewell Tour* comes from popular media and social media; it sneers, preens and insinuates. None of this is accidental. Mohamed is a skilful poet with a brilliant knack for refashioning the rhetoric of disposable media into lines which convey an extraordinary energy; but the true purpose of these poems is moral. We are shown the ugliness of our culture. In some places the ugliness is replicated within the poems, but what we also get is some of the sharpest satire and most inventive writing you will find in any book published this year. This is not a melancholic book of disappointed patriotism, lamenting what has happened to our country; it is an outpouring of disgust at the people we have become. Brilliant and horrible in equal measure." - Tom Sastry, author of *You Have No Normal Country To Return To* and *A Man's House Catches Fire* (Nine Arches Press)

"It's rare to feel the thudding sadness and crumminess of England skewered with such elan. It's a bit like coming home from a few nights in literally any city on the continent, no actually, literally any city in the world, still high on their grace and multiplicity and public luxury. And then having to spend ninety minutes on a carcinogenic Tube train next to a man eating a whole chicken with his hands. But what I want to suggest to you is that that's good, actually, and cathartic, or enematic, and somehow in the slew of everything that suffocates every spark of joy, invention, hope or transfiguration, Stefan Mohamed locates a *via negativa* towards something better." - Luke Kennard, Forward Prize Winner, author of *Notes On The Sonnets* (Penned In The Margins)

"Cheeky, observational and deliciously apocalyptic, Stefan Mohamed's *Farewell Tour* is a surreal, satirical road trip of a collection that's as sharply funny as it is disarmingly beautiful. I never wanted to get out of the passenger seat." - Molly Naylor, author of *Whatever You've Got* (Bad Betty Press)

"*Farewell Tour* is a road movie crossed with a fairground ride: thrilling loop-the-loops of language plus a sense of dangling over a frightening drop. As playful as it is smart, this shape-shifting state of the nation satire never lets us rest. Like a hall of mirrors it bring us face to face with grotesques we recognise, horribly, around us. And look, some of them are ourselves." - Philip Gross, Bloodaxe Poet, TS Eliot Prize winner, National Poetry Competition winner

"In this refreshingly deranged concept collection about navigating an unwelcoming England through internet din, Stefan Mohamed commits to a dark comic vision with a vengeance. Among swerving perceptions and punchlines, we get poetry like sweets in a glove compartment: 'a treasure trail of road signs rendered meaningless in the blink of deep time'. If you've ever dreamt of finding a work of wild verbal satire in the little free library 'on Discrepancy Close, Battleborough'... you're already lost in the world of *Farewell Tour.*" - Jeremy Noel-Tod, *Sunday Times* Poetry Critic, Associate Professor - University of East Anglia

Stefan Mohamed
Farewell Tour

VERVE
POETRY PRESS
BIRMINGHAM

PUBLISHED BY VERVE POETRY PRESS
https://vervepoetrypress.com
mail@vervepoetrypress.com

FIRST PUBLISHED SEP 2022

Printed and bound in the UK
by ImprintDigital, Exeter

ISBN: 978-1-913917-13-5

To everyone out there
doing good things.

CONTENTS

Acknowledgements

Farewell
Tour

Road Trip

You are having another stupid argument, loudly, over coffee. You are arguing over whether it's possible to download a haunted map. You firmly believe that it is not. That only the physical can be haunted. That only the analogue can trap a ghost. They insist that no, code can grieve. Even ones and zeroes have unfinished business. 'Error 404' is just the machine's way of requesting an exorcism. You are stubborn. They are forthright. It is as it always is. Construct. Cold open. Delivery system. Two best buds on their first big adventure. Two fiery lovers grasping for clarity. Spouses, comfortably fading, on a final quiet pilgrimage. Estranged siblings paying off an unspoken debt. Strangers united under the unlikeliest of circumstances. It doesn't matter. Who you are, what scars or supplies you bring to the table. Travel sweets, cigarettes, war stories. Haunted maps. None of your fashionable *motivation*. None of that *context* the kids are into nowadays. None of that enervating trauma. Just the journey and the land. This sinking land, this drowning land, this haunted, haunting, cursed and cursing land. This stubborn rainy kingdom of cracked breezeblock and deflated swamp. This sulky empire, primarily exporting derivatives, entropy and bad vibes. Call it an end-of-the-road trip. Call it a farewell tour. A last hurrah for a collapsing island. The map, whether beamed to your phone's cracked screen or scrawled, scrunched up and left yellowing in a glove compartment, is spectral either way. An order of service for a state funeral. No special announcements. No lessons. No catharsis. Just a steady fading to an unsteady rhythm, and a treasure trail of road signs rendered meaningless in the blink of deep time. You can't wait. You're excited beyond reason just to get out of the house.

Itinerary

You will cut like crows
through the heart of Marmite County
from Oodle to Mashing
to Gossip to Pummelling
via Bishop's Heartburn
then onward to Halfwick, Beleaguer
Dimmington, Dogdiss
Heckhorn and Illtide
with a stopover at Queen's Complaint.

As sun pours sickly
over The Stales
you will wind a figure eight
between Axebury and Battleborough
past Cravendale and Grimmouth
via Big Bungle
(avoiding Little Bungle for obvious reasons)
through Pissing and Thwacking
then onwards to Quim.

Breakfast at Pustule
lunch at Drubbing
dinner at King's Nob.

Another early start
the long Southern Road to East Northwest
quick stop for a selfie at Folding Hill
brief detour taking in all the Burnt Edges

(Upper Chuck, Lower Cuck, Fitherstowe,
Crumplebottom, Ivyrash, Leching, Lubberdean
and Lossford)
then an unfulfilling night at a grubby b'n'b
on the cusp of Great Rot.

Leisurely scenic route to King's Trauma.
Brunch at Jumble-on-Sail.
Avoid Oakmember and Rashgate.
Slow down to take in Stable Hill
but definitely don't stop
because it's going to disintegrate
any day now.

Afternoon tea at Rimwell if you're on schedule.
Service station pasty if you're not.

Then onwards
to Snarlingham, Shufflebum and Slugley
past Trilling, Tetchy and Titchy
through Version, Diversion, Inversion
and Upper Lowington
with a brief detour to West Wanging
then up and over the Great Yommon
to Little Vile
and Bad Crumpet.

Dinner at Brittleton
a mediocre guest house at Upper Yeeting
then up bright and early
to bend a windy descent to Swimmer's Ear

where you will park the car
and with much ceremony
hurl yourselves into the waiting arms of the sea.

Marmite County

you either love it

narrow as a vote, noble as a knife, face of a
hawfinch, teeth of a hen, knees all clotted
with sycamore cream, hurling back pints in
the White Tailed Eagle, lines of Charles II
with Autumn Blaze Maple, addled adders
older than alders, living colours with ugly
heads, business-cold and proud as dogs,
sweating like a disco in a Transit van, uncle
of a colonel screaming "Punch And Judy
Cancelled?!", Spotted Dick vs Eton Mess -
Live At The Rootless Cosmopolitan, Lucy in
the Sky with the Kitchen Sink, Suffragette
Sue and the Rich Tea Biscuits, Robin
Hood gritty reverse-genderswap reboot
controversy, TARDIS full of stolen Irn
Bru, Round Table hangover, Camelot
cramps, scarecrow tears, the Phil Mitchell
Curse, eat the mushy peas when the man
is green, pay Walrus and Gumboot for
services rendered, *wicked! wicked! Lidl is
massive*, white poppy pudding with traitor
glaze, *The Culture Show With Cultural Norm*,
Glastonbury casualty, Holby City Rollers,
Mog Gets Fleas, so solid croon, two
thousand different words for 'arse', sunsets
to have your heart broken by, a heron

down every chimney, ASBOs for dreams, laughing in the face of league tables, twee as a jackboot, the new grime monarchy, the old punk lobbyist, banter with the lads at the Sunday Roast, dead of an Elizabethan haemorrhage, paralysed from the top hat down by a quirk of common fate, sarcastic to the last, loser celebrates first, nice hot cup of aggressive self-deprecation, illegal caravan rave thwarted again, families and fields, blood and pavement, campfire curses, car park hymns, who stuck 20p in the village idiot, doomscroll nailed to a faded oak, drunk on sunset and puking on moon, cool wet dirt too fresh for your nose, gravel after a pissed-off rain, kooky quagmire country where the birds are always bickering

or you're broadly indifferent

Short Cut

(overheard in a Little Chef twelve miles outside Bishop's Heartburn)

If you're so bloody clever why didn't you carve
the map into your *face* and then maybe we
wouldn't be so lost

I'm sorry
but this has not gone according to plan.

I could not have prepared us more thoroughly
for this quest.

I maxed out our inventory
with vitality potions, holy elixirs, 4D crystals,
cybernetic elbows, petrified tentacles, temporal
gems, paradox pants, sentient amber,
chameleonic ammo, self-replicating paninis,
enchanted story tapes, infinite bumbags,
and everything else we could possibly need

while you just
kind of
ran around in a circle.

I single-handedly raised our stats
plugging away for hours in
the Screaming Fields, the Copse of Corpses, the
Chaos Barn, the Homicide Bog, the Mirror

Mansion, the Cancer Library, the Multi-Storey
Graveyard, the Murder Wedding, the Goblin Off
License, Satan's Leisure Centre, and every other
mind-bending gauntlet of horrors on this
miserable map, mowing down hordes of swamp
nerds, scum lords, flaming farmers and rotting
councillors

while you just
kind of
glitched in and out of some scenery.

I navigated us through
hysterical villages, treacherous river crossings,
fraught encounters with former allies turned ene-
mies, thematically resonant tests of
fortitude, multi-stage battles with recurring
nemeses who *kept on cracking out a new form*
just when we thought we'd finally killed them,
all those poorly-timed captures and hair-raising
escapes and revelations that entirely re-
contextualised all that came before, not to
mention the thousand or so interminable side
quests in which we helped old men find their
favourite saucepan or whatever

while you just
kept spunking our hard-earned currency
on escalatingly ridiculous outfits
that you never wore more than once

and d'you know what
the least you could do
is keep hold of the map
i.e.
the one thing
I asked you to look after
you complete
and total
ANUS.

I'm keeping the Experience Points.
OK?
OK.

National Anthems (Mixtape)

1: Remember When Dogs Were Wolves

2: Remember When Cats Were Wolves

3: Remember When Binmen Were Wolves

4: Remember When Wolves Were Mental

5: Remember Battery Lickin'

6: Remember Shadow Gropin'

7: Remember Fibre Snortin'

8: Remember 10-Day Weeks

9: Remember Bleak Weekends

10: Remember Numb Honeymoons

13: Remember When Wet Was Dry

14: Remember When Soft Was Hard

15: You Weren't There

16: You'll Never Understand

Pub Grub

Queen's Complaint
an upscale downmarket town
nestled in the cradle
of two separately disputed valleys
boasts 1,066 individual pubs
within the municipality.

Notably
389 are called The Red Lion
while 346 are called The Royal Oak
and 331 are called The Crown.

More notably
you have been banned
from all of them.

Seditious banter.
Aggravated hustling of a new pool table.
Jukebox hogging in the second degree.
Ordering gender-inappropriate cocktails.

Nevertheless
you're going to try and get served.
Into one, into all.
A pub is holy ground.
It cannot reject those
who seek sanctuary.

You know this to be true.

It's in the Magna Carta.

Advanced Planning Theory (Audiobook)

The great urban planners of the new century imagined municipal transplant loops, extensive zoning conflagrations, multi-speed traffic sandwiches, infrastructure dissolution, superstructure reification, diffusion of key distribution networks, non-linear street hierarchies, chaotic neutral real estate, restrictive easements, inequitable reversals, surrealist land allocation, CO_2 emission reduction as free jazz, human geography as hardcore punk, landscape architecture as spacious dub experiments, public administration as unhinged hip-hop screed, public consultation as John Cage's *4'33"*, rethinking prisons through the prism of Gershwin's *Rhapsody in Blue*. They imagined extrapolating the optimal layout of targeted green spaces via a kind of reverse hauntology practised only by the very serious monks of the central planning committee, a confidence trick that looks like managed decline and sounds like managed decline and feels like managed decline but will assuredly lead inexorably to utopia, recycling one hundred TVs to build fifty slightly nicer TVs, draining the river every Christmas Eve and refilling it with slightly less of itself, building inwards to build outwards. They imagined innovative subterranean micro-boroughs with a different corporate sponsored algorithm representing every square inch, parking tickets you can eat, parks you can keep in your pocket, pockets you can keep your brain in, brains you can balance your coffee on, coffee in the water fountains, coffee in the fire hydrants, these great men and women and neither and either and other of the new era, dreaming nightly of a world in which nobody need ever again say *don't talk to me until I've had my coffee*, because nobody will ever have not already had their coffee.

Tourist Information Board, Cravendale

The town expresses both the jubilation and the terror inherent in creation. It suffocates in treacly kitsch. It dreams up a fictionalised shoreline and becomes almost anonymous. It stems from the same irreverence that animates an audacious young squid. It has burrowed itself into the consciousness of a critical hall of mirrors, an all-time hall-of-fame joke. It proved highly relatable to a lot of other nobodies.

The town wasn't a winning formula commercially. It barely keeps the sadness at bay. It is almost painfully unremarkable. Its manipulated fields provide a fascinating new way to understand life. It jettisons used memories and sounds more resigned than outraged. It isn't concerned with projecting any sense of rustic authenticity. It flirts with the public consciousness, takes various reference points and has some healthy fruits to bear.

The town was a deciding factor in how the final circus left. It leaves behind very little evidence, but you can still see its names on Google Maps. It is weird, beautiful and repugnant. It's going to haunt the story. Its suitably eerie nature builds on contradictions, where people rain all day but dust doesn't settle. Its textures are structurally and technically operas; the palate feels strangely intimate.

The town is not a human settlement. It shares an origin with a fortress or enclosure. It is not a reliable determinant of cultural characteristics. It does not discriminate between autonomy and language. It was intended to be self-reliant, but was not successful. It was not allowed legally defined boundaries. It is largely unwritten. It has at best a questionable claim to be called a town. It provides the concept of a town.

Clowns (Mixtape)

1: Clowns bewildered by a relatively straightforward logic puzzle

2: Clowns unexpectedly aroused by the tranquil beauty of nature

3: Clowns exhausted and hormonal having spent too much time with infant clowns

4: Clowns driven to distraction by toddler clowns

5: Clowns at a firing range

6: Clowns at the DWP

7: Clowns practising squirty flowers on a street corner

8: Clowns frustrated by clown police broadly miming at them to move along

9: Clowns discovering other clowns floating face down in shallow water

10: Clowns ambivalent as young adult clowns leave the circus for the first time

11: Clowns joylessly fucking to pass the time

12: Clowns trying to perform their usual act wearing plague masks

13: Clowns hurling themselves poetically from white cliffs

14: Clowns leaving drunk replies on their old ringmasters' Instagram posts

15: Clown, aged and pale, unable to place the smell of greasepaint, telling anyone who will listen that they were once able to fit 30 people in the back of one car, calling all their flappy -footed grandchildren by the same name, the name of a clown who died half a century ago, and who nobody else remembers

Traditional Pub Menu

Starters

Colonial hooligan bantering on a bed of
redacted wince

Common hubris with Jerusalem cul-de-sac,
gammon libel and green unpleasant hills

Vindictive maypole deep fried in vague
embarrassment, with flag *ennui*

Small grey headaches braised in tatty nostalgia

Toasted poppy, served with poppy-fried poppy
and fizzy poppy cordial

Mains

Fish empire locked in a headache of grey
motorway

Crippling pagan canal with jailed sheep and
loutish gravy

Wet green bulldog with repressed ham

Perfidious tradwife on a bed of nervous
Morrissey, with rose vomit and corrupt ale

Balding village with fag butt lager, bleak beans
and stale emojis

Strolling violence, slow cooked in legitimate
concerns, with fucked pebbles and strained
patter

World cup, with your choice of world wars

Desserts

Meadowsweet bantz with tired old pride and
white noise

Mean-spirited queue baked in walloping
Thames, with flaked cronyism and stone circles

Hard border stewed in damp class system

Toxic Y-fronts with guilty seaside and White *Vin*
Man

Victim complex baked in sloppy denial, with
custard

Rural Continuum

You are having another exchange of views, frankly, over the roar of the engine. They keep calling this place, this rolling mess of hills and trees and contradictions, this trick of old-fashioned back projection held together with sawdust and gallows humour, a country. But the first thing to say about this country is that it wasn't conceived as a country at all; they call it a 'continuum' because that's what it is, a mess of warring tribes who have somehow managed to hold it together for nearly 20 centuries. Most of the time they're barely keeping up with geography's ceaseless forward drive. Often they find themselves sitting at the top of a hill, enjoying a fondly remembered view for the first time, not just figuratively, but often quite literally, because everything below them has somehow moved, and nobody saw fit to ask their opinion, and suddenly they are those people, demanding the return of a place that they cannot prove they ever really visited, but instead of gunpowder and a sword, all they have is a Facebook group and a drink problem. You stop for breath, and they ask you how you can possibly say you don't believe in ghosts. And even though you never actually said that, you decide to let them have this one.

Fragments of Radio Interview
with Former National Treasure

so are we not allowed to say we love it

WHAT IS IT THAT YOU LOVE

we must take it. warts and all.

it is a place whose idea of itself bears no relation whatsoever
to the data we have available

one has to laugh, really

as you make your way quietly and
methodically to the designated end point

TRANSCRIPT OF A
FREE JAZZ BANQUET

pathetic little spat-out

nugget of

sewed up my own

mouth to stop

it has the

constituent parts of

you can always find

something to love

but

that doesn't mean that you

have to

let yourself

*tried the fine selection of herbal
teas but*

NONE

THE

WISER

I have found exactly one workable method

of squaring the whole thing and I am more

than happy to pass it on to your listenership

I hope that it helps to

s t a

t i c

suppose we may as well put on some music instead, few hours left until
sunrise and this is a very creepy bit of motorway

Armageddon Outta Here (Mixtape)

Intro: Keyboard Warlock - 'A Flower Running For Cover' / 'Shopping Lists For Shops That No Longer Exist' / 'Unplug National Psyche And Plug It Back In Again' (Medley)

1: Wisdom Tooth Drum - 'Glass Three Quarters Empty (The Quarter Is Where It Gets Interesting)'

2: Unmarked Envelopes - 'The Cat Who Only Seems To Be Around When Somebody Dies'

3: Tongue Half-Bit - 'A Tooth From The Gob Of Every Cop Who Tried To Stop You Walking'

4: Brainworm Fortress - 'Pour Me A Shot Of Collective Blood'

5: Confiscating Dreams vs Crack Lullaby - 'A Bell Falls Off A Clock And Lands In The Long Grass'

6: Homeless Ghost - 'Jigsaw Puzzle Pieces, Unevenly Redistributed (Out Of Context Remix)'

7: Silly Mr Baby - 'You're The Only One Who Can Make Sense Of Thunderstorms (Robbie Strawberries' If It Ain't Broke Don't Fix It Re-Fix)'

8: Flagged For Inappropriate Content - 'I'm Not
Sure How To Frame This Collapse, Whether To
Locate It Within A Narrative Or To View It As An
Observable Accident; There Is Very Little
Mileage In Blaming The Gods, You're Never
Going To Get Up There To Have It Out With
Them, I'm Sorry But You're Just Not (Parts 2-4)'

9: Fallbackposition - 'This House Has One Room
And It Doesn't Fit'

10: Rattled By The Lack Of Urgency - 'I'm Just An
Ant, I'm Just A Crow, I'm Just A Cardboard Box
With Nothing In It, Questioning Its Position In
Relation To The Rest Of The Physical Universe,
No Biggie'

11: Airplane Mode - 'Longer As A Cog Than
As Debris'

12: The Church Of Proper Closure - 'Making A
Noose Out Of Jokes'

13: 11+2 - 'Track The Thirteenth (Between
Twelve And Fourteen Variations)'

14: Genocide Amendment vs Johnny
Warcrimes- 'The First Duty Of Government Is To
Protect Its Citizens'

Poem To Be Whispered Tenderly Into The Ear Of A Stranger Bleeding Out Outside A Kebab Shop At 2am

I was a flower of the greasy spoon, yes!
When I put the Marmite in my hair
like the girls from Greggs.

Or shall I wear Heinz Baked Beans?

And how he kissed me
under the low wall
round the back of the Co-Op.

And I thought, well!
As well him as another.

If Pat Sharp leaves his fun house today
he will find Dave Benson Phillips
seated on his doorstep.

If Blobby goes forth tonight
it is to Noel his steps will tend.

Every life is many gungings
day after day.

We gunge ourselves
gunge robbers
gunge ghosts

gunge giants
gunge old men
young men
wives, widows
brothers-in-law

but always
getting our own back.

God made PJ
the devil Duncan.

And it is as painful
perhaps
to rhumble
as to get ready.

Architecture

Your brutalist cottage is just this map but real.

Tower block auras are real. You came from a cave, brought a book called 'The Charm of Old Stones'. Hopped between losses with unthinkable ease.

Heritage walk at famous Aesthetic Age 'loss tower' is cancelled until further notice.

Futuristic student accommodation proudly trumpets its skeleton of native infrastructure. Nobody notices the discrepancy.

Not one of the twelve murders supposedly committed on Discrepancy Close, Battleborough, has ever been officially confirmed. Its status as a 'fractal cul-de-sac' is also disputed.

John Fractal's Post-Post-Post-Post-Modernist 'House That Cannot Physically Be Lived In' may be an architectural dead end, but that doesn't negate its value, suggests the cover feature for this month's *Degraded Utility*.

Like many modern degradations, the gentrification of oxygen is just one of those

things we haven't got the time or space to
worry about.

Magpies

You are having another debate, spiritedly, over layby kebabs. Roadkill shish. You are debating the significance of magpies. You always salute them, just in case, a habit drummed into you by *mamgu*, who taught you no birds in the house, no shoes on the table, salt over the shoulder. Who taught you *hiraeth*, one word generations deep. A key to crack the code of future grief. One for sorrow, she taught you, and you clearly remember a single magpie regarding you with sombre button eyes through the church window, weeks shy of turning eight, as you sobbed into your order of service. You insist that it must mean something. They ask why it should. Not unkindly. Two for joy, they say. *So why did two watch from the power lines when I found my dog dragged bloody across the road, mangled and left to die?* You laugh at the casual brutality. Nod and shrug and change the subject. Don't eat any more. And in the privacy of memory you remember *three for a girl and four for a boy, and five for silver and six for gold, and seven for a secret never to be told,* and as you pull out onto the road you see eight lined up to see you off, and you smile and salute. Your companion does the same. No more is said.

A green and pleasant break

(to be declared aloud by Richard Burton
and no-one else)

And did those great puzzles
in ancient weekly
win big cash prizes?

And was the holiday in Greece
with brother's best mate's stepdad seen?

And did the little boy divine
scream forth as I gave birth?
And was the bravest mum-of-six
run over here?

Bring me my 30-minute meals!
Bring me my secret lover!
Bag me my bargain: oh clouds unfold!
Get my hubby pregnant then marry me!

I will not cease from mental fight
'till we have built Jerusalem
for under £1.

Normal Island

(watched idly in a supine state on a TV in a dingy Travelodge)

It's the nation's favourite sitcom! Colonel Bumbridge-Tuft blusters a racist diatribe at Priscilla's wedding - chortle or cancel? Bad Luck Laura has been trying to apply for housing benefit since Series 3 - will Series 81 finally see her triumph? Ernie Crabs the lobbyist's son harbours dreams of poetry - we love to watch him fail! 'Patel' the plucky asylum seeker has survived torture, unfriendly oceans and more torture - now he must try to find his way to the local Job Centre, with hilarious consequences! Wee Jimothy Pimothy lives in a cupboard, and there he should stay! The Chancellor of the Exchequer eats a cat live on TV and his approval rating just keeps climbing! Daisy Estate is crowdfunding her mother's kidney transplant! Maisie Tate will have her revenge on the plebs! Granny T smokes 400 cigarettes a day and punches cows at the weekend! Grandpa D has monetised his insomnia! Tessie tends her vegetable patch to tune out the noise! White Collar Greg has friends in high places! Steve the Spiv 'loses' those pesky contracts! Middle Class Mike, the landlord's landlord! Cheeky Oliver scrunches himself into a ball and gets stuck in a pipe! Angela Terf-Hypocrite gets into a sticky situation down at the bowls club! Local DJ Mickey Knobs destroys the big wedding - and not in a good way! Baby Cheese builds a twin out of garbage! Princess Binky falls in love with a portrait of herself! Ken Bozo has been licking the same stretch of pavement since Episode 2! Kev Peaches is in another castle! Gavin the Swamp King begs delivery of 1,000 rare monkeys to his dilapidated squat - a cliffhanger for the ages! The new novel from Millie Bellams is a slab of collapsed void that lies dormant if unobserved, but if read will expand exponentially and consume all around it - a plotline that viewers will find 'confusing' and 'off-putting'! Bob Girth has doorstepped 99 grieving families without suffering violence - will number 100 finally deliver the goods? Dilys Crunchy refuses the call! Busby Morgan reuses an egg! Kip Fraggle eggs a binman! Trash Milligan kips in a bin! Alison's nightmares are too real to handle! Millicent's handles are a real nightmare! Tom Toad hires a creepy face in a puddle to fiddle his accounts! Bill the border guard is just doing his job! Sebastian Fashley runs for prime minister by accident and reintroduces capital punishment on purpose! Every day, Floppy Freda gets off the train at Debacle Central - but not today! 'Asif Thingy' is the best kind of immigrant, his neighbours agree! The Shadow Minister for Authentocrat Posturing marries a poppy wreath and adopts a pork pie in a doomed attempt to appeal to the working classes! Byron Bumfluff gnaws off his own legs to make a point - will it be heard? Mr and Mrs Curtain-Twitchly would rather die than see a single person get something for free - tonight, we'll put their resolve to the test! Silly Harry gets sent to the Tower for sneezing near the King - villain or menace? Silky Sally once showed some cleavage at the school disco - harlot or harridan? Find out in tonight's thrilling season finale! Series 82 starts tomorrow! Series 83 starts the day after! Don't look away! Don't you bloody dare!

Dawn Chorus

it is a privilege
quiet and enormous
to walk alone at sunrise

dewdrop crystals lit up
all alien
and chiming

blood sorbet
on a bed of onyx
and chlorophyll

blackberrybird harmonising
a tiny xylophone
in its throat

shards of moon
still humming
prayers

secrets held frosty
in stasis
like spiderwebs

evaporating
upon
contact

Maggot Mondays

(Viral post on Rural Instagram)

Rise and grind, time to eat that Monday!
Fill your cheeks with cherry pips
and spit 'em in the moonshine bucket!
Deflate the tractor and fold him away
'til winter!

Bumfluff Bill bought a cow to surf on!
The distinctive trilling call of the Feathered
Karen welcomes you to the meadow!

Rise and grind, time to squeeze that Monday!
Strip the bark from Uncle Tree
and make a summer suit!
Build a hay bale Babel Tower
and begin your ascent!

Kiki Pith sowed a poem into the wheat field!
The Morris boy's vibrant plumage has everyone
at the barn dance hot and bothered!

Rise and grind, time to kill that Monday!
Time to peel off the cellophane sky!
Time to do the maggot waltz!

Jacky Ladders uninstalled the moon!
Lucy Broom knocked up a new one!
Nobody will know the difference!

TripAdvisor Review - King's Trauma

Took the Hitler Bus to Atrocity Park.

Kittens crying from burning trees.

Blood cookie picnic on the bigot platform.

Low effort zombies pulling teeth in flooded
living rooms.

Mangy drones raiding the suicide bins.

A bulldog named Bailiff chewing on a landmine.

Tiny skeletons welded to a radioactive slide.

Trying too hard. Unlikely to go back. Toilets very
well maintained. 2/5

Traditional Joke Formats

i.

A bad workman walks into a bar carrying two
birds. He speaks to a drowning man, a fool with
money, and a one-eyed doctor who claims he
can keep the blind away. The workman puts
both birds in one egg, which he puts into two
baskets, which he throws over to the other
side of the fence. The bartender asks what he
wants to drink. The workman says *'cowards cross
streams where they are shallowest'.* The
bartender asks him to leave, and he does,
quietly.

ii.

An idle devil in a deceptive workshop kills a
chicken with a cat. The cat says *'don't bite off
more hands than you can swallow'.* The devil
doesn't listen.

iii.

Beggars seldom lay golden eggs, but cannot
choose when they do. Have you ever seen it
happen? It's hilarious.

iv.

Don't count your bridges. I counted all mine
once and was bed-ridden for days.

v.

Real babies throw out their own bathwater
and make sure not to take themselves with it.

ambient noise

migrant hits wind turbine. wind turbine shuns language. illegal UFOs pour in. enough is enough. illegal UFO takes our country up the aisle. illegal UFO paralysed by language. if the UFOs pour in today will the last person to leave please grab the crown jewels. enough is enough. will the last person to leave please paralyse the UFO. migrants fired for being UFOs. how many more can we take. enough is enough. squatter holed up in yer allotment. UFOs terrorise yer allotment. abolish yer allotment. yer potty plan for world peace. up yours. enough is enough. we must stop the language invasion. 4,000 foreign languages we can't throw out. 500,000 foreign languages get social housing. murderers get social housing. UFOs get social housing. hamsters get social housing. enough is enough. is THIS the most dangerous hamster in our social housing. UFOs ate my hamster. hamster ate my Michael. Michael ate my George. George ate my social housing. zip me up before you go go. enough is enough. new fears over illegal hamsters. hamster who made love to pavements. George's brain is missing. UFO horror show. hidden hamster millions. how do you solve a problem like language. every four minutes a UFO arrested in our country. enough is enough. I saw Hitler fall out of 70mph car and bounce down the M1. this one's for you. hamsters take ALL new jobs. slash benefits for hamsters. slash benefits for UFOs. slash benefits for Hitlers. enough is enough. fury at Munchkin Maggie. stick it up yer Hitler. we've all been screwed by the ding dong song. a sea of white flags. bin bagged. enough is enough. world's tallest migrant has landed. Is THIS the most dangerous migrant. migrants in yer allotment. war and pizza. queasy does it. hamster invasion will start riots. red line on hamsters or else. enough is enough. UFO leaks gas. yer language leaks werewolves. it's language wot won it. army spot migrant hamsters over yer allotment. strangers in our own allotments. sling yer hook. enough is enough. the oompah strikes back. gotcha. enough is enough. werewolf seized in our allotment. enough is enough. wrong foot in the grave. enough is enough. werewolf immigration horror show. werewolf backlash. enough is enough. werewolf 'swarm' on our streets. enough is enough. UFOs set to flood in. enough is enough. Easter outings werewolf threat. time to bite back. send them all back. brave moo world. crust ahead. enough is enough. war on woke wind turbines. war on woke werewolves. war on woke hamsters. woke hamsters' potty plan for world peace. war on world peace. war on language. enough is enough

City Break, Snarlingham

Preening, vicious
and defined by a gleeful antagonism
your urban staycation
promises a mashup of provocations.

You will gawp in delight
at the city's primal thrills.
Aggro and oddly utopian
the danger of collapse is part of the fun.

The accommodation is all edges
a flourish of serrated design
and detuned boundaries.
Cacophonous mutant caves
marked with cruel symbology.
A distinct sense of elitism.
No patience for heritage.

You will find yourself subsumed
in an atmosphere
of relentless momentum.
Come for the pure virtuosic fear
and the frenetic consciousness.
Stay for the sense of jittery drama.
Doomy and unfashionable.
A series of happy assaults
that pass, in the right light
for a unified vision.

Reflecting on the legacy
of multiple, interminable wars
you will walk the oozy streets
snapping selfies against the grayscale gothic
tagging the pictures *bleak*
and *murk*
and *mire*.

Tech bums on Hawaiian beaches
will heart react.

You will miss the feel
of air.

Bertha Benz (Audiobook Preview)

The world's first recorded long-distance road trip by automobile took place in Germany in August 1888 when Bertha Benz, the wife of Karl Benz, the inventor of the first patented motor car, travelled from Mannheim to Pforzheim and back in the third experimental Benz motor car (which had a maximum speed of 10 miles per hour) with her two teenage sons, but without the consent and knowledge of her husband. This radical new adaptation of the classic historical footnote reimagines Mrs Benz as a sort of proto-girlboss, a Strong Female Character before there were Strong Female Characters, a Manic Pixie Dream Suffragette, a human Rosetta Stone for contemporary liberal feminism. This road trip will have action. Intrigue. Suspense. And, most importantly, the immutability of biological sex. We have instructed our writers not to look any further into Mrs Benz. She no longer belongs to herself, to her descendants, or even to history. She belongs to us.

Poem To Be Bellowed From Car Window While Hurtling Down A Hill At Unsafe Speeds

Who are you saying is *dead*?
What would you classify as *dead*?
In this scenario, is agriculture *dead*?
Is the soil *dead*? The land *dead*?
An excess of nation *dead*?
Chauvinism *dead*? Status? *Dead*?
Is the general notion of civic virtue
and group dedication *dead*?
Is classical enlightenment *dead*?
Robust obligations? Minimal samaritan
responsibilities to foreigners?
Are these things *dead*, in your hypothesis?
Devotion to a sense of place?
A sense of life? *Dead*?

Is sovereignty *dead*?
Are territorial authorities *dead*?
Symbols? Myths? Traditions? *Dead*?
Unified community? *Dead*?

My dead hand my dead tongue my dead rain my
dead garden my dead rivers my dead currency
my dead ancestry my dead air my dead-

*(At this point, the car should hit a tree at sufficient velocity
that all on board are fatally injured)*

Retirement Community, Tetchy

They use feathers from broken-down birds
to make their cages smell of home.

Abstract and perfect.
Something beyond nostalgia
that cannot be compromised.

They use bones too
as a kind of *feng shui*
scraps of flesh still attached

> *this is my cage*
> *violently won*
> *and I will dismantle*
> *all intruders*

a table of bequeathments

> *self-destruct buttons*
> *hostile architecture*
> *someone else's ration book*
> *the space where the ladder was*

and beyond, a lawn.
Not a blade out of place.
Poppies and barbed wire
and a sunken-eye Churchill
drooling foamy blood.

On a clear day, you can hear tea pouring.

You can taste expensive glass.

You can smell the hate.

Toponymy

Your genes derive from a disputed tribe
made popular on a poetic island
whose oldest proto-human bones
were constructed from clay.

Your geological composition
is one of the most dynamic in the world
and your free market principles
affect people and goblins
up to the age of 19.

Your Renaissance forcefully asserted
bad co-ordination, stormy weather
and the decline of the native red squirrel.

Your prisons play a key role
in meeting energy demand.

Your traditional festival
is famously controversial.

Your elements are the most useful
reference system in the world
providing valuable insight
into your psychology.

Your names
can be difficult to interpret.

You know they're political
and why
but you will die
before you explain yourselves.

Britpop

(To be dreamed while driving at night)

You are hungover in an aggressively generic greasy spoon, sweating into your scrambled eggs. You twitch a peek over the rim of your Royal Wedding mug and choke down a gob of horror: the other patrons are lumbering, inky black squids, moist and shiny, pulsating with suckers, balancing awkwardly on their plastic stools, trying unsuccessfully to hide behind their procedurally generated tabloid newspapers. One of them is wearing a bowler hat at what you assume is an alien squid's idea of a jaunty angle. You catch its eye, its grotesque glassy plate, a porthole into a swirling, unfathomable web of mind. It looks... smug? Satisfied, even? You look down at your mug. It is not clasped in a hand, but wrapped in the glistening black of a tentacle. 'Roll With It' by Oasis starts to play. *You gotta-*

You are propping up the bar in an aggressively generic pub, trying to order a pint, flailing your moist, clumsy tentacles. You're not sure if it's your inherent lack of charisma that's stopping you from being served, or the fact that you haven't mastered this new body, or the fact that the other squid have no qualms about pushing in front of you. You're also aware that there was no transition. You were in the greasy spoon, now you're in the pub. There is a football game playing on a big TV, squid ambulating gracelessly back and forth on a pitch that looks like it needs mowing. From the stands, a group of lairy squid fans launches a full-sized sperm whale onto the pitch, and the squid players swarm towards it, buzzing furiously. In the pub, the atmosphere changes. You finally manage to get the bartender's attention, and order whiskeys, vodkas, lagers and ciders for everyone. A cheer goes up from waiting squid, and somebody puts a song on the jukebox. It's 'Tubthumping' by Chumbawumba. *I get knocked down, but-*

You get up off the floor and immediately vomit extravagantly into the bowler hat of a visibly impatient squid. There was no transition. You were in the pub, now you are in an aggressively generic alley somewhere, violently emptying your cephalopod guts. Fully voided, you pass the hat back with a slurp of apology and trundle unsteadily down the road, trying to recalibrate. Routemaster buses, Morris Minors and Reliant Robins full of squid pass, eyeing you accusingly. *But why*, you think. *Aren't I one of you, finally?* You are twitching, paranoid, thick viscous globules of perspiration dripping down your leathery hide. You pass a busker, who is also a squid. They're playing 'The Scientist' by Coldplay. *I'm going back to the-*

You are hungover in an aggressively generic greasy spoon, sweating into your black pudding. You twitch a peek over the rim of your *Beano* mug and choke down a gob of horror: the other patrons are humans, undignified sacks of pale, quivering flesh with tiny pig eyes, balancing awkwardly on their plastic stools, trying to hide behind their procedurally generated tabloid newspapers. One of them is wearing an I <3 [Insert Nation's Capital] hat at what you assume is a tourist's idea of a jaunty angle. You catch its eye, its tiny sneering pinprick. It looks... superior? Knowing? You look down at your mug. It is not clasped in a hand, but wrapped in the glistening black of a tentacle. For some reason, this fills you with relief, but it is short-lived, because suddenly the other patrons, the squishy pink piles of blob with their angry breakfasts and novelty mugs, are surrounding you. They press inward, a solid wall of accusatory flesh, reaching out with their horrible scissor fingers and peeling off strips of your lovely shiny squid hide, like they're disassembling a jigsaw puzzle depicting something they'd rather not share a towel with, tossing scraps of you over their shoulders for their little yappy dogs to catch. It hurts, but in the same way a confirmed suspicion does, which is to say, bearably. The theme tune from *The Archers* starts to play. You decide to just roll with it.

Traditional Folk Poems

(reconstructed by the Anthropology Dept. of the University of Bad Crumpet)

i.

old corrupty crow dog
whittles back knots
where the woods go dark

duke o' bloody baths
all a-cuckoo in the water
with his egg un-yolked

chickenworm begotten
of a fresh black mould
sicken of a dance

all o' these three
in crack-a-back tree
sleep silently

all o' these three
in crack-a-back tree
sleep silent, see

ii.

oil feather fiddles
on bitch-burn rock

buckin' in a puddle
with a witch-black sock

easy if a-nether
get a-bitten by a bee

waspy 'n a willow
wi' me wife's old feet

iii.

o where be my wee Doris to?
found her in the butter
with sticky-lip mouth

o where be my wee thiefling to?
strap her on a birdie
pack her off south

o where be my wee griefling to?
where be she?
be she true?

Dead Villages

The internet has discovered a blog post
written by your travel companion
when they were younger
and much less guarded.
The red flags are at full mast.

The hive mind calls the post 'graphic'.
'Controversial'. 'Divisive.'
For nearly ten thousand raw and twisted words
your travel companion
describes *a journey*
taking in one hundred dead villages
arranged at astrologically significant intervals
along the living spine of this diseased
and crippled country.

They've had all the blood mined out of them.
Bone marrow extracted by committee
and left to expire on darkened shelves
limbs discarded in cornfields
twisted in balloon animal knots
stuffed into the hollows of ancient trees.

The further they travel
the more these villages seem to resemble girls.
Girls with *thatched-over eyes*
and lips of coal

girls strangled by anonymous metal-glass gleam
dumped like trash
and called trash
beneath memorial Facebook posts.

Parts washing up all along the river.
Puffy green flesh. Coughed-up worms.

People are demanding reparations.
Spitting ultimatums.
Malicious re-litigation
in the kangaroo court
of the comments section.
Ambiguity is anathema.
People want room for misinterpretation
but not that much, for God's sake.

What are they *saying*?
Is there something amiss with our menfolk?
Or is it the young people who are wrong?

You venture the question.

They say, eyes on the road
and casual as you like
this country hates its girls.
This country eats its young.

This country cannot live with itself.

A Complete History of the Contemporary Now - Revised Edition

(You genuinely planned to read this in the car)

Remembrance (sacrifice)	**250**
Remembrance (slights)	**252**
Newspapers (bile)	**280**
Newspapers (news)	**299**
Jarmindy Cribbyn	**300**
Traitors	**350**
Cry laugh emoji	**390**
More memes	**420**
Statues	**430**
Gammon (slur)	**500**
Nightmarish hallucinations of Maypole dances soundtracked by grotesque remixes of traditional folk songs	**550**
Jabberwocky Crabbinges	**555**
Paranoia	**570**
Sex (lies)	**600**

Pint Glasses

You are sparring, fondly, over pints. There are
beautiful days, they say, often, but that's why
ugly hits like it does. That's why the granite
mornings and the bugbears on toast and the
rainy fascism of a Tuesday morning cut the way
they do. Leaving just enough flesh on the bones
to deny the mercy of numbness. You smile and
laugh and toast the hyperbole, and from the
empty half of your glass you pull memories and
premonitions, sacred and casual and pleasantly
messy - click of pool balls, snap of ring pulls,
frosted window, sizzle of sausages on bank
holiday afternoons. Smiling at strangers under
quiet skies. Kissing under umbrellas while the
rain tries its worst. And they're not getting it
right now, but there is space in their glass for
more.

**Poem Constructed From Every Pregnant
Silence When You Almost But Didn't Quite
Speak Up Because Of The Threat Of
Violence Hanging Over Proceedings Like
A Fog, Hot And Red, Gripping Your Glass
To Stop Your Hands From Shaking, Staring
Into The Bubbles, Breathing Silently,
Avoiding Eye Contact At All Costs,
Withdrawing Into Statue Safety, Waiting
For It All To Blow Over, Please Can It Just
Not Kick Off For Once, Please**

Catharsis

You are having another circular discussion, quietly, about closure. Crammed into a cramped b'n'b bedroom, absorbing old sitcoms, puddle of tea, faggots and gravel and pesticide crumble. You are both avoiding the window, your portal to the edge, where the land surrenders to the sea. It's just dirt becoming water. It tells you nothing. And all these pictures. Seasides and sheer cliffs. Gardens, dogs, gardens, seasides, ladders, ruined castles, smashed up kebab shops, dogs, seasides. They tell you nothing. Certificate of authenticity for a Ford Melancholia. Signed replica of Eric Morecambe's famous glasses. Lyrics to 'All Things Bright and Beautiful' written on shells from various beaches. Print-out of an article from a long defunct zeitgeist-y culture dispatch offering a comparative analysis of a brutally quashed socialist uprising from the late 1800s and an illegal rave from the early 1990s where DJ Leveller played the entirety of Thatcher's 'The Lady's Not For Turning' speech over the extended mix of 'Let Me Be Your Fantasy' by Baby D and was subsequently beaten so savagely by riot police that she suffered permanent brain damage. VHS of old *Countdown* episodes, including the infamous incident where the word girl accidentally spelled out a rude word and was subsequently outed as trans by a vengeful tabloid. They tell you nothing. Disintegrating copy of a banned *Beano* annual in which Gnasher eats a Polish migrant. It tells you nothing. Tonight you will sleep in a bed that feels like a failed marriage. Tomorrow you will fold yourselves back into your car. You will stop briefly to look at the sea, then head for the border and escape none the wiser. But you will be gone. You will have tried. And you will be together.

Fish and Chips (at Swimmer's Ear)

The salt is eroding you.
Chipping off
that aggravated shell
invisibly formed.
History and
other sediment.

Salt
lifted from the ocean's
freezing face.
Hurled like a spell.

Salt
pleasant and bitter.
Like glass
smashing against your teeth.

This is not a tender exchange.

The sea is tactless
the wind impatient
the rain an indifference of blades.

The process
if it can be called love at all
is its final, toughest form.
Mostly bracing.

Your ears hurt
your eyes are red
and the numbness
goes deeper than bone.

But the car is warm
the flask is full
and the tape is in

and you are clean
and raw
and ready.

Tape

With warped sigh and faint corroded hiss
you stitch a magpie mess of static ghosts.
A knowing smile and warm *remember this*
a tapestry to soundtrack fading coast.
Somehow it fits with this eccentric space
this haunted, haunting, cursed and cursing isle
frozen mid-decay, rigid held in place
with rituals of sacrificial bile.
Your haunted map is exorcised, for now
an armistice for temperamental ghouls.
Another ritual. A quiet vow
to have another crack with better tools.
    The road signs start to blur, then disappear.
    The future needs to eat. Don't interfere.

ACKNOWLEDGEMENTS

I had no idea if this book was going to work when I started writing it - looking forward to finding out - and I'm very grateful to everybody who has taken the time to read it, offer feedback and confirm that it is, in fact, something.

Thanks to Ross McCleary, Tom Sastry and Beth Cochrane for their essential notes on the project, particularly comments like 'this line is great' and 'hahahaha'.

Thanks to Stuart and the team at Verve for believing in the book and putting their energy and resources behind it.

Thanks to Luke Kennard, Molly Naylor, Philip Gross, Jeremy Noel-Tod and Tom Sastry (again - I definitely owe you some pints) for saying nice things about the book for us to put on the cover.

Thanks to my family and friends for the constant validation.

Thank you for reading the book. Please follow me on social media, like and share my posts, subscribe to my YouTube channel, sign up to my Patreon and so on, as I also require the constant validation of strangers.

ABOUT VERVE POETRY PRESS

Verve Poetry Press is a quite new and already award-winning press that focused initially on meeting a local need in Birmingham - a need for the vibrant poetry scene here in Brum to find a way to present itself to the poetry world via publication. Co-founded by Stuart Bartholomew and Amerah Saleh, it now publishes poets from all corners of the UK - poets that speak to the city's varied and energetic qualities and will contribute to its many poetic stories.

Added to this is a colourful pamphlet series, many featuring poets who have performed at our sister festival - and a poetry show series which captures the magic of longer poetry performance pieces by festival alumni such as Polarbear, Matt Abbott and Imogen Stirling.

The press has been voted Most Innovative Publisher at the Saboteur Awards, and has won the Publisher's Award for Poetry Pamphlets at the Michael Marks Awards.

Like the festival, we strive to think about poetry in inclusive ways and embrace the multiplicity of approaches towards this glorious art.

www.vervepoetrypress.com
@VervePoetryPres
mail@vervepoetrypress.com